App Development

App Design and Development for Beginners

Rob Justice

Table of Contents

Do you even Code?

Today it's hard to point out an activity we don't have an app for. Eat, sleep, exercise, date - you name it, there's an app for it. And yet people come up with new apps that cater to needs we haven't even thought about sometimes, every single day. Free, high quality apps have become pretty much the norm. What brought about this tide of apps?

Increasing literacy of coding. **Programming literacy is the literacy of the 21st century.** We're making more and more digital devices and programmers are the ones building interfaces for us to control them. That's why people with programming knowledge are highly valued. Look around, the mean salary of a programmer in the US in 2013 was about $ 80,000!

Programming languages of old like C, Objective C that are strongly-typed, hard to understand and pretty much limited to nerds are giving way to newer ones such as Python and Swift which are easy to learn, require less typing and are much closer to natural languages. So, more people learn them, look around for ways to make lives easier and create wonders with the power of programming at their fingertips.

Quite a lot of programmers are only involved in creating apps for mobile devices. It's easy to learn how to code for mobile phones, and you know how many people use a mobile. Create an app that will smartly help people do something easier than before, maybe make it something completely novel and voilà! You're the creator of the next million-dollar brand!

Programmers are proud of the fact that they can command a digital device and bend it to do their bidding. Non-programmers are lesser mortals in their eyes. But hey, programming isn't that hard! In fact, they try to hide how easy it is. If everyone learned a language, they won't be so special anymore will they?

And with this book, you're going to make a mobile phone do what you want. You're going to show them that you're just as capable of taking control. You're going to become one of *them*.

But no, **this is not your handbook to learn a programming language.**

We can tell you where to learn from, but teaching a language is out of the scope of this book. We'll teach you how to choose which platform to build for, how to organize and go about the building process and what to do to release your app.

Apps, Applications and Software: They're not the same!

What's in a name? That which we call an app, by any other name would function the same. But there's a reason why all these words exist separately. Software is the common term used for all forms of instruction sets that control digital hardware. There are two types of these; system software and application software (or just applications). System software include operating systems and other programmes that directly control hardware. Applications run on top of those and perform specific tasks like playing music, browsing the web etc.

Apps are simply smaller forms of applications (like the word itself). There are many forms of apps that run on a plethora of devices from mainframes to mobile devices. We're concerned with what we use daily – mobile phones. Hence, apps naturally mean the applications that run on our smartphones and tablets.

So, apps are basically a subset of applications, which are in turn a subset of software. This means that apps are small pieces of software written for mobiles. Shakespeare wasn't wrong, he just didn't think of set theory.

Android and Apple – The Two Realms

Which one should you first develop for? Or should you go for something else altogether? Currently, **Android and iOS account for more than 96% of the smartphone market share**. That's right; Windows Phone, Blackberry OS, Tizen, Ubuntu for Mobile, SailFish OS all make up less than 4% of the global smartphone operating system market. Talking about Windows Phone, it's the distant 3rd in terms of OS market share and even Microsoft isn't sure where they're headed – they cut off nearly 7800 jobs just in July, and wrote off $ 7.6 billion spent mostly on acquiring Nokia. It's obvious that you should start off with the two titans, at least for now.

But which one first? That decision depends on a number of factors including your budget at the starting point, your target audience, profitability if you're planning to make money through the app (like In-App Purchases), the trouble you're willing to go through to release the app etc. Let's go through each carefully, better know what you're getting into before rushing in blindly and getting lost.

Target Audience

Android commands a gigantic 81% of the international smartphone OS market, running on all kinds of hardware from cheap disposable phones to high-end offerings like the Samsung Galaxy S6 Edge. On the other hand, iOS runs on around 15% of the handsets, but they're all high-end devices.

The story doesn't end with just those numbers. Research shows that iOS customers generate more revenue for developers than Android users, even with the lower user base. More on that next under profitability.

Different markets are dominated by different players. For example, most developing countries have more Android users due to the sub $ 300 mean asking price of Android handsets. Comparatively, iPhones have a mean price tag of $ 600, making their way more into the crowd of developed countries. People of certain countries have special preferences too – Japan has an even number of iOS and Android users but Spain firmly nods at Android with 90% to itself, leaving iOS to make do with a meagre 8%.

Another point of view on the target audience is the level of hardware needed to run an app. If you're making a super heavy app that needs a lot of resources and powerful hardware, it means you're targeting the high-end devices. Going with Android for a large app will result in a lower market penetration as nearly two third of them are mid range or lower devices. But iOS runs on iPhones and iPads which are all high-end. If you're targeting maximum market penetration, make an app with a smaller hardware footprint for Android.

Bottom line - consider where your app is going to be used and look which OS is dominant there. And don't forget to think about what kind of hardware your app requires. Always look into the target market demographics before making an app.

Profitability

You can develop apps for money, or you can do it as a hobby for personal satisfaction. It's another way to serve the community at large. You can start off by developing apps for problems you see in your day-to-day life and then share them with people around the world. I remember one mother who created an app to help her autistic son communicate. Having started off as a personal solution, today it helps the lives of thousands of autistic children and their parents around the world. Doesn't it feel great to know that you are helping some stranger in a far away corner of the world, touching their lives digitally? If yes, just skip this part!

Apple's App Store generated 70% more revenue than Android's Play Store in 2014, according to the Analytics firm App Annie. And that was with less than one fifth of Android's market share.

Being expensive brings Apple devices a certain level of exclusivity to a class of people that are well-off, which naturally translates into more spending ability in the App Store. iOS apps consistently show better revenue when compared to their Android counterparts. The spending habits may be equal among flagship Android phone users and iPhone users. But when taken as a whole, it's quite obvious that the not-so-well-off majority of Android users are reluctant in spending money for apps and in-app purchases. **(In-app purchases are the stuff like coins and extra lives, keys to locked content and some limited services of apps and games that you can buy within the app. Payment is done with a credit card registered with the relevant app market or by carrier-billing.)**

At this point you're right to conclude that iOS is the path to a higher revenue. But it's wrong to generalize the results of overall store revenue for your app. What you should do is comparing the figures of apps similar to yours, at least by category if not by the apps individually. Check the price, number of downloads, implementation of in-app purchases and differences of such apps and then decide which platform looks more profitable to you.

Initial Budget

While both platforms allow developers to build apps for free, making a payment to release them is a must for iOS apps.

Android developers can easily get all the developing tools they need for free and run them on all major computer operating systems. Google even provides them with certain free testing tools and online resources to manage apps, like the Google App Engine. But **you need a Google Play publisher account to release apps to the Play Store, with a one-time payment of $ 25**. This isn't an issue if you host it somewhere else, i.e. this is not a compulsory cost.

It's not exactly that easy when developing for iOS. First of all, **you need a Mac with OS X** if you're serious about it. Virtual machines will work but you really don't want to do that, for reasons we'll discuss later. So first there's the cost of the Mac. Once you have that, you can develop iOS apps with free tools provided by Apple. The next major obstacle comes when you try to get your app into the App Store – **you need to become a member of the iOS Developer Programme, which costs $ 99 per year**. The sad part; hosting it somewhere else is useless – read app release procedures below.

Yeah, it's kind of expensive for the total noob. But there are very valuable facilities provided to members of the developer programme, like getting support from Apple's own crew of iOS technical support engineers. You'll learn more about these as you read on.

Ease of developing

Both platforms have dedicated tools for developers to code an app.

Needless to say, you need to know the relevant programming language to do so. For Android, you need to know **Java**. Apple has its own language called **Swift** for iOS app development.

Each language has its own strengths and weaknesses, which will either make your life easy or miserable as you use them. One point worth mentioning is that Java has applications outside of mobile developing as well.

Android has Android Studio as the standard IDE (Integrated Development Environment) from Google. **Apple's solution is called Xcode**, which is much older than the Android Studio and arguably better in terms of user-friendliness and functionality. Both offer options to create graphical user interfaces and interactions but with the years of experience under its belt, Xcode feels much more polished. Overall, it's generally accepted that Xcode is the easier environment to build apps with, at least until the Android Studio catches up.

But the latter already has the upper hand when it comes to app configurations. It provides a neat list of permissions for each app when compared to the cluttered, exhausting list of build settings that Xcode shows. You'll see how irritating a single tick can be.

Something far more important is the OS fragmentation of Android. Being free and open, Android runs on hundreds of hardware configurations made by a number of manufacturers. When a new Android version arrives, most of these devices are not updated because it takes a huge amount of engineering resources and time to customize its base source code for each hardware configuration. Hence most manufacturers only update their most popular handsets, leaving others stuck in some older Android version. This requires developers to code their app for multiple versions of Android if they want to reach a higher user count, making the development process quite hard. This is without even thinking about the myriad of different screen sizes with the same internal hardware.

Apple designs and manufactures iPhones on their own and as such they are in total control of both the hardware and the software. Additionally, they only make a couple of devices per year – there are only 20 Apple mobile devices in total as of July 2015. This allows Apple to easily update and maintain their devices, which translates into a higher number of iDevices in the latest iOS version. Hence developers can easily develop for a single iOS version with fewer screen sizes and still reach a far higher number of users.

App release procedures

Google's process for Android app release is quite open in comparison to the tightly controlled, closed approach of Apple regarding apps for the iOS. You don't even have to release an Android app on Google's own Play Store; either distribute it personally with the setup file, via another Android app market like Amazon App Store or Xiaomi market, or officially release it through the Play Store.

In the case of iOS apps, you're only allowed to release them through the Apple App Store. For that, first you need to get approval for your app through a review process too. You can host your app somewhere else but quite often only jailbroken devices will be able to install them. If you know what jailbreaking is, then you know this isn't the best way to publish an app.

Too much technical jargon? Relax, learn about them bit by bit. There's a panoply of things out there to make your life easier as a developer, you just need to be patient and willing to learn. Read Harry Potter? There's a golden line in the 5th book which applies to programming wizards as well. It goes like this;

"Every great wizard in history has started out as nothing more than what we are now, students. If they can do it, why not us?"

- J.K. Rowling, Harry Potter and The Order of The Phoenix.

Time to grab your wands, or rather the keyboards in our case, and do some magic.

The Wizard's Magic Satchel – What's In It?

Know what a magic satchel is? No, okay I'm just being fancy saying this is what a mobile developer has; you'll need these to be an Android or iOS app developer.

Proficiency in the language specified to develop for each platform.

A system with the minimum requirements to run the developer tools.

You'll also need an active internet connection to download the developer tools and search online each time a bug comes up. And that's going to be almost always.

There are platforms like Xamarin which allow you to code for both iOS and Android at once, but they often run into issues which leave even experienced programmers dumbstruck. Coding out of the native environment and languages leads to instances that are hard to explain and you're better off without them, at least until you change the beginner status.

Let's consider each platform individually.

Android

As we mentioned before, the programming language for coding Android apps is Java. It's a child of the C language, but much easier to handle. The official developer tool is the Android Studio. Here's the list of stuff you need to start coding.

1. Java Development Kit 7 (or higher, latest at the time of writing this book was JDK 8)

This is available at

http://www.oracle.com/technetwork/java/javase/downloads/index.html

1. Android Studio
2. Android Software Development Kit (or the Android SDK)

Find these last two at https://developer.android.com/sdk/index.html.

But before downloading any of these, check whether your system has the following specs to run the software. These are the common system requirements for running the Android Studio on Windows, Mac OS X and Linux.

- RAM: 2 GB minimum, 4 GB recommended
- Free Space: 400 MB for the Android Studio
- At least 1 GB for the Android SDK, emulator images and caches
- Screen resolution: 1280 x 800 minimum

Apart from that, there are some OS-specific requirements as well.

- Windows - you need to run Windows 8/7/Vista or Server 2003 (32 or 64 bit versions). Note that Windows XP is not supported. Time to move on, buddy.
- Mac OS X
- Version 10.8.5 to 10.9 (Mavericks) are officially supported.
- Java Runtime Environment (JRE) 6 is required in addition to the JDK.
- Linux
- GNOME or KDE desktop
- GNU C Library (glibc) 2.15 or later
- Ubuntu 14.04 Trusty Tahr has been the test subject for Linux based systems. So you're more unlikely to run into errors in that.

You probably don't need much help if you're already running Linux.

Note that these are the confirmed-to-work system configurations listed for the Android Studio. Other operating systems such as Mac OS X 10.10 Yosemite are also known to run the Studio but they often cause errors. If you have a different system, it's better to look around and confirm that you can run it, and that there are enough people like you to ask for help if something goes wrong.

The latest Android SDK is automatically installed when you install the Android Studio. But if you're going to build for older Android versions, you'll have to download the individual SDKs for them. There are some system requirements for installing the JDK as well but they're automatically covered by the above so we won't talk about them.

You might have heard about the Android Developer Tools (ADT) and Eclipse IDE being used to build Android apps. This was the combo for that purpose for quite a long time, but using Eclipse proved to be frustrating and Google saw this problem. So they quietly worked on creating their own IDE and that's how the Android Studio came to be. It's based on the immensely popular IntelliJ IDEA, the Java IDE by JetBrains. It's out of beta phase now so you'll encounter far less bugs. You can still work with the original tools but keep in mind that Android Studio is now the official tool for Android app development, and **Google has announced they'll end supporting the ADT** plugin for Eclipse by the end of 2015. After that it'll be only maintained by the developer community. Why waste time on tools destined to be soon obsolete when you can use the official, recommended software? Let's be future-proof.

While that covers your developing requirements, releasing an app to the Play Store needs the aforementioned Google Play publisher account with the $ 25 payment. Again, this is a one-time payment, which is a bit comforting compared to Apple's annual charge. Information on app distribution on the Play Store can be found here. There you will see exactly what you need to do to sell apps or give them for free. Don't forget to check the lists of supported countries for each option.

Alternatively you can host your app somewhere for free or release it via other app markets like Amazon app store. Amazon doesn't have any initial charge for publishing apps via them. They just take 30% of the listing price per each sale. Go to this web page https://developer.amazon.com/public to publish via the Amazon app store.

Here's a list of resources to learn Java if you're a complete beginner in programming.

- Android Tutorial for beginners – 3 parts.

- Java for complete beginners – Cave of Programming

- Android Studio Training – Google

This is the definitive guide on using the Android Studio. But you need to know Java first.

iOS

We already mentioned that developing for iOS has a higher initial cost. First there's the fact that you need a Mac. Then you need to be a member of the Apple Developer Programme to publish your app. The programming language is Swift, which is a hybrid language based on Objective C and inspired by Python & many other languages. All the work is done within the Xcode IDE owned by Apple.

- **Any MacBook Pro will run Xcode** and let you develop apps. But try to get one with at least

  - an Intel Core i5 processor

  - 4 GB of RAM

  - 128 GB SSD

Any used Mac that can run OS X 10.10 is good enough, but it's better to steer away from the MacBook Air series. If you're on a tight budget, a well-configured Mac Mini will also serve you well enough. It starts from $ 499. The higher each of these specs, the better. But you don't need a Mac Pro, that's like hiring Beyonce to sing a lullaby – insane.

Another option is coding with Xcode on a virtual machine. A virtual machine runs on the resources allocated to it by the host system, and the host system itself needs some resources to run. This translates into extremely slow operation in a normal PC. It'll be hard to get past coding as a hobby with such a system. So virtual machines are not recommended for iOS developing unless you have a monstrous workstation or gaming rig.

Xcode 6.4

- Setup Size – 2.61 GB

- Requires OS X 10.10 Yosemite or later.

- You can download this from the Mac App Store at https://itunes.apple.com/us/app/xcode/id497799835

- Make sure you have at least 5 GB of free space, you'll need more as time goes on and you work on more projects.

- Other resources needed to code like SDKs and the Swift Compiler are bundled into the Xcode setup so you don't need to download anything else like the JRE for Android. But developing for older versions of iOS will require you to download separate SDKs, just like with Android.

Xcode is the IDE for developing for iPhones, iPads, iPods, the Apple Watch and Macs. So getting into iOS developing marks the beginning of developing for all the Apple devices. As you advance in your programming life, you'll find yourself building beautiful apps that work across the width of the whole ecosystem of Apple. Sounds exciting doesn't it?

Objective C was the language previously used to build apps for iOS and Mac, but now Swift is replacing it for iOS, OS X and WatchOS apps. Obj-C is quite verbose, having its roots in C, and 3 decades old now. Apple wanted to create a higher-level language that is easier to handle, has the advantages of Obj-C and is modern. After years of development, we see the result as Swift. For a brief description on the differences between Obj-C and Swift, go to this link. Swift is the future of developing for Apple so by all means spend your time on learning it.

There's just one more hurdle you must know about – gaining membership of the Apple Developer Programme. There are actually two roles in developing for iOS ; being a registered Apple Developer and being a member of the Apple Developer programme.

A registered Apple Developer account is only enough to *develop* apps for iOS. It is free to register and you get access to all the latest developer tools including Xcode and SDKs, documentation and tutorials etc. Registration is done with an Apple ID at the following link.

http://developer.apple.com/programs/register/

You can provide an existing Apple ID you use to make purchases on iTunes and the App Store, or create a new one altogether by selecting "Create Apple ID". Once you do that and provide necessary credentials, the next page presents the Apple Developer Agreement which is of the usual user agreement format. But take your time to go through their conditions. Mistakes aren't that hard to make. After agreeing to it, you're taken to the Apple Developer Member Center home page. Do not mistake, you haven't enrolled in the Developer Programme yet. Here you can download SDKs and submit bug reports, it's all pretty self-explanatory.

Apple Developer Programme facilitates distributing apps through the App Store. As mentioned earlier, this costs you $ 99 annually but gives access to much needed facilities as well. The foremost example is the ability to test your app on physical devices. Certain parts of apps like TouchID authentication, In-app purchases, location services etc. require a physical device to be fully tested for proper functionality. A full list of Developer Programme membership details can be found here.

If you need more help on choosing a membership, check out Apple's support page.

And here's a list of resources to get you started with developing for iOS with Xcode and Swift.

- Free Udemy course – Beginner iOS Development.

- Xcode and Swift tutorial for beginners.

- iOS Developer Library - has everything you might ever want to know about developing for iOS.

o Tutorial on developing iOS apps

o Apple App Distribution Guide.

Especially, read the guide for configuring your Xcode project for distribution. It's important for testing and releasing your app.

A few tips to the new followers of the path...

1. Take your time to learn things carefully.

You can learn a programming language's basics within 4 weeks. But don't think that it means you've finished the language. Modern languages have so much to learn that require years of practice. You won't even hear about most of them until you have to actually use those parts at some point and search for them. Remembering all of it is also impossible due to the sheer amount of things. You'll just have to look it up when you need something rarely used. So every programmer needs to be ready to search for stuff and understand them fast. It takes nearly a decade to truly master a single language so as to call yourself an expert in it; you gain knowledge as you go forward.

2. Go through each and every example and RUN IT.

It's very important as a budding programmer to carefully examine the examples of language usage. Try to guess what it does before checking the result. No one gets it right all the time at the first go. More importantly, you should not read it and just think "oh, I get that. It's easy. I'll just use it when I need it." It's nearly impossible to remember exactly how a certain method works without having tried it out first. So, manually type as many examples as you can (no copy-paste, don't cheat yourself) and let it burn into your memory.

Then try using those methods for something similar in logic to the example but different in its application. Even if you receive a piece of code from someone else, try to construct your own method of achieving its purpose. This is very important for beginners. Sometimes it might not be possible to come up with a totally new solution, but at least try to evolve what others give you. That's how you *learn*, folks. You need to be patient to do things properly.

3. Understand what's happening behind the scenes.

You really won't get anywhere good if you blindly use existing methods without understanding what's happening in the background. Let it be a simple print statement or something a little more challenging like quicksort, you need to understand how you're getting the required results. That way you'll know how to achieve something, where to look in case something goes wrong and get better at combining methods to get a particular result.

Your understanding of methods of coding and creativity are what give birth to better implementations of a language. If it's extremely good, you might even get to name a specific method after you. It's going to be legendary.

1. Learn from experienced people, and don't believe it right-away when someone says "this is the best way to do that".

Each person teaches you according to their own level of expertise. They're only as good as the level they're in right now. Naturally, people who have been coding for years will know more than your friend who took a Computer Science class in high school. So try to clear your doubts from someone far ahead of you, someone who has a lot of experience as a developer. This also means that you should not hold on to someone's advice as the ultimate truth or the word of god. There may be better ways of doing something which they simply don't know.

A very good place to get answers to your coding problems is <u>Stack Overflow</u>. It's a question and answer site maintained by developers for developers. You can post a question and attract answers from experts in the relevant topic, and others will vote on them to give you the best answer. First look into frequently asked questions to avoid duplicating a previously asked question.

1. Check out other people's code.

There's a lot you can learn by looking at how other people achieve things, especially experienced programmers. You can learn different programming styles, learn new applications of methods, find new methods and so on. Try to pick up good programming habits like proper indentation, documentation, commenting etc. But never get used to the bad ones such as impromptu variable names or functions. Get involved in open source software projects and see how people collaborate to make universal software.

<u>GitHub</u> is a repository hosting service with many open source software projects that you can peek into. It's currently the largest code hoster in the world. Sooner or later, you'll create a GitHub account and make use of their tools too.

1. Teach others what you know.

Teaching is a very good method of solidifying your knowledge. You don't have to finish learning a language to teach something about it to someone else. I have a friend who makes programming tutorials while learning different languages. His latest blog post was "Things I wish someone told me when doing Haskell" and it included solutions to things he got frustrated with while learning Haskell. For this he first learned that language, encountered problems, figured out how to solve them and then presented his solutions in a form easy to understand. This process makes him think on his own and research, adding up to a better knowledge of the language. You should see the advantage of this; it makes you confirm what you learn, leave no grey spots in your knowledge. Less "that might work. I haven't tried it though" moments.

Design and Develop

Contrary to the popular belief that programmers are messed up and work all over the place (well, yeah but not in *everything*), they're quite methodical when it comes to their job. There's a standard order of doing things when you write a programme, called the Software Development Life Cycle or the SDLC. Originally intended as a guide for writing PC software, this is more or less the same for mobile developing too. There are 5 major steps in the SDLC of an app.

1. Define your idea.

2. Design the visual elements.

3. Develop the app.

4. Test your product.

5. Release and maintain it.

This covers everything from having an idea for an app through coding it to finally bringing it out to the world. Sometimes you'll find yourself working on multiple steps at the same time. This is just the accepted way of doing things, how you might *expect* to work, but you're free to go however you like. In fact, this particular SDLC is commonly known as the Waterfall model. It features a sequential approach to developing software, like the steps in a waterfall. There are many other models like Spiral and Agile but assuming that you're a beginner working on your own, waterfall model works best. Time to get to work!

1. Define Your Idea.

It doesn't matter if you woke up with the idea for the best app ever or thought about it while waiting for sleep to embrace you, the first thing to do is defining what you're going to make. So a computer is not your first tool, grab a pen & paper and sit down. Take a deep breath (really), and answer the following questions.

- What is your app going to do?

What's the primary purpose fulfilled by the app, is it solving a current problem or introducing something new altogether? Write down if you're making a remote controller app for a spaceship or making a new Tetris version.

Having a clear purpose is extremely important, especially in the case of iOS developing. Apple will reject your work in their review process if they deem it to be unsuitable for the App Store. It's better to go through their <u>Review Guidelines</u> now before spending months on something only to face rejection.

- Are there similar apps for this purpose already out there?

Check the app markets to see if someone already came up with that idea. If yes, next check if they're doing well. The number of downloads and user reviews should help. Then figure out how you're going to differentiate your app, or whether it's not worth working on anymore.

If you decide to go forward, well now those existing apps will actually help you. If the current solutions don't have favourable ratings, learn where they have gone wrong. User review section is a gold mine for this. See what people hate about those apps and check what the most requested features are. Then try to incorporate those into your app. See, you're already better than them.

If any of the above apps are free, try using them yourself and carefully examine what's good and bad, which parts can be improved or whether your idea seems pathetic compared to their solution. Don't feel bad, try a thousand and one ideas. Try to do something better. You have to succeed only once.

Differentiating your app is crucial for success. You need to be able to say why your app is better. Offer something more than the rival apps. It could be a new function or an easier way of doing something. Sometimes you can charm users with a great interface that does less then the others, but the main purpose well.

Note that I am not asking you to sit down and come up with an idea. It should be something that has already occurred to you. Sitting on a chair and trying to force out ideas will not result in anything *great*, because you're trying to come up with something just for the sake of doing it. Use that idea which already *hit* you while doing something else. There's a real requirement there, a real intention of solving a problem.

- Exactly how will it work?

You need to have a clear idea on how you get each bit of functionality offered by the app. What are the libraries you're going to use? Are there any special algorithms? What kind of a back-end is required? Will that function work as intended on all target devices? What should the target device have to use the app? Will it be using content already available? If yes what are their sources? The answers to these questions will give shape to your idea.

A very important fact to consider is whether you can actually implement the functionality you hope to offer. This depends on 3 factors – your ability as a coder, the time you have and the budget. Certain bits of functionality may require a higher knowledge than you already have. You can either spend time on learning what's needed, or pay someone else to do that part for you. But don't be too ambitious. Some tasks will require knowledge and practice gathered through a few years to code. Stubbornly trying to learn them fast and do it yourself will not yield a quality product. This might hurt a bit, but either buy or cut off the functionality that you can't offer within a reasonable time period. Please don't lie to yourself, be realistic.

Having a proper time frame for your project is the next step in the definition phase. A little bit of self-induced stress can do wonders in terms of productivity. Create a small set of milestones (say, you'll finish the UI by this time, finish location-based functionality by this date and so on) and work on them one by one. This should be done after deciding on what your app will do and how you're going to do it, because time requirements depend on the functionality of the app.

Creating a very simple prototype at the beginning is common in the SDLC, even though coding is the 3rd step in the cycle. This helps you to form a rough idea of the outlook of the app and makes it easier to design it. It should not get too deeply into any feature but act as a dummy for you to work on through the SDLC.

Done defining your app? All right, time to use your art boards next.

2. Design your app.

Let's note something important before going any further; the design of an app docs not define its functionality. Functionality and the target system define the design. You can think of wonderful design features to add to your app but are they going to look good and work well in a particular device? For example, split-screen multitasking works fine on a tablet but a regular mobile phone's display is too small for that.

Certain features like real-time search results look simple in design but require hours of intricate programming to implement in the developing process. Hence the developer and the graphic designer should communicate in very specific terms about the design and functionality. First decide on what the app will do, then choose a suitable design for it. NOT the other way round. The target system's hardware limitations should also be considered in a design. A device with a less powerful chipset might not work seamlessly with certain features.

The visual elements of your app take form in the design phase. This is where you'll decide what buttons to use where, how colourful they should be and their size etc. But first, we need to create a flow of functions that feel natural and easy to access to the user. The technical term is a Flow map, which is a graphical representation of the flow of functions from the central view of the app.

Think of Instagram for an example. In the main interface you get a few basic function links – Home, Search, Capture, Notifications and Profile. Tap one, say Profile, and you come to the user profile where you can find profile-related stuff like the ability to check older posts and edit profile details. If you tapped on Capture, a new page appears with options to select a photo from the Gallery or snap a new shot. Let's look at the flow of functions here;

Main interface >> Profile >> Edit Profile >> Change user name

Main interface >> Capture >> Select from Gallery

You can see how they begin from the main interface and *flow* on to different functions within the app. This flow of functions is called the Flow map. We draw this with bubbles and arrows starting from the main interface in the centre. It has no visual elements yet, rather it defines in which order the visual elements should let the user control the app. Note how key features are higher up in the hierarchy, i.e. closer to the main interface. Each first option corresponds to the foremost functions a user can perform, and all the other functions are divided into different levels under them in a logical manner.

The first layer or level of functions lead to secondary functions under them, and so on. This creates an intuitive flow of commands that the user can follow with ease to achieve a particular purpose. It's important that you first spend time on creating a logical navigational structure with a flow map before designing any UI elements. Actually this is a part of the UX.

Now to the mysterious UI and UX designing. UX means Ụser

Experience, while UI stands for Uers Interface. There's actually a subtle difference between the two terms, Even though they are mostly used interchangeably today. The user experience design takes an analytical approach to the organization of visual elements of a particular product whereas the user interface is directly what you see from the outside, what we interact with through taps and swipes. Confused? Let's try the Instagram example again.

In Instagram's home screen, you can scroll up and down to view different content, tap on home to return to the top and tap on other icons to go to different parts of the app. And in the home screen, shortcuts are given at the bottom of the screen as a set of tabs. Notifications is a different type of info, photos are another, you get the picture. The information within the app is separated appropriately – there's an architectural design in the presentation of information. We call this the Information Architecture.

The scrolling action, the shortcut dock and the categorization of information are all part of the UX. It dictates in which order the visual elements are shown, what they do and how they are enabled etc. It aims to to improve the user's experience in using the app by presenting a satisfactory combination of functionality and ease of use. Check Don Norman's original definition of it sometime.

The UI comprises of the buttons, colours and animations etc. of the app. It's the skin, or the cosmetic outer layer upon the bare bones of the UX. This is where the graphic designer gets into the play. But before designing any graphic content, you should know that there's a distinct style of graphics and how they should be used in each of Android and iOS. These are called their design philosophies.

The design philosophy of Android is called the Material Design. It was introduced by Google at the Google IO 2014 as a *"design metaphor inspired by paper and ink that provides a reassuring sense of tactility"*. It uses flat visual elements while mimicking the natural flow of things in the real world. The Material design is so powerful that even websites ended up adopting it soon after its introduction (a recent adopter is the web interface of WhatsApp). You can get the official guidelines for using it at the Android Design page. There's a ton of free resources too, ranging from colour palettes to icon collections.

Apple's design philosophy doesn't have a particular name. But almost everything they do have always been strikingly beautiful, elegant and simple. This is seen in both their hardware and software designs. The definitive guide to achieve the proper Apple look is given under the iOS Human Interface Guidelines.

Both companies strive for simplicity and are strict in their design policies, Apple a tad more so than Google. You should always create an app that looks consistent with the rest of the particular platform. Otherwise the interface feels out of place and may confuse the user into uninstalling it. People expect the same visual quality from an app as the native system applications. A well-planned, beautiful interface keeps the users hooked onto what they see on screen. The look and feel of your app will make it or break it, regardless of how well it functions.

We're done with the flow map, know what kind of a look and feel we're going to give your app and now it's time to draw the actual elements. First you draw a *wireframe* depicting the static shapes and placement of elements in the app's interface. Work on it through a few iterations until the interface seems satisfactory. Get the comments of a few other people as well, this will help you to avoid the pitfall of thinking your design is perfect. It's others that are going to use your app, you should learn what they want it to be like. There are tools like Lovely Charts and NinjaMock that let you easily create wireframes for free.

Graphic designing is a separate field in itself which has a myriad of things to learn. You can either study the design guides yourself and use tools like Adobe Photoshop or GIMP to create the necessary content. A much easier way of getting things done is hiring a freelance graphic designer. Sites like Fiverr and Upwork have hundreds of experienced graphic designers who will provide you with great designs fast, for a fair price. If you choose to do things yourself, try the Creative Bloq for tips and resources.

Buy and play Monument Valley to see how beautiful an app can be. It's a game so you won't see any design guidelines being used though. Games don't exactly need you to stick with guidelines. Note how the graphic designer uses mind-blowing art to entice the player.

Using hamburger menus:

There was a time when all apps came with hamburger menus hiding their functions. These allow a lot of options to be crammed into a separate instance of the interface, hidden behind a small icon with 3 lines that look like a hamburger. Also known as the navigation drawer or sidebar, this was later proven to negatively affect the user experience.

People weren't mindful of what was hidden behind it. This translated into less user engagement as a whole, which is detrimental for an app's success. Simply put, what's out of sight is out of mind.

Tech companies were swift to take action when research revealed this phenomena. So they came up with a design that was much more visible and consistent, something that kept the top features on top of the user's mind. This is the tab bar, the one we see in all major apps today including Facebook, Twitter and Instagram.

Of course, it devours a bit more screen real estate. But this can be easily made to hide when the user is concentrating on the content, thereby minimizing the effect on screen area. Try to include 4 key functions (maximum 5, the icons shouldn't be too small so as to misplace the tap on them) separately in the tab bar and hide the rest behind a hamburger menu.

The choice to use a hamburger menu or a tab bar depends on the functions of the app. It makes sense to hide the secondary stuff behind a sidebar if the app has a clear cut primary function that can be used directly, like an app for the FM radio. Sound settings and saved stations can be put behind a hamburger. Google's own Play Store app still uses a hamburger menu for accessing the user account and apps etc.

Whatever the designs you use, the maximum file size for an Android APK is 50 MB, but you can attach two expansion files which are limited to 2 GB each. iOS apps also have a total size limitation of 2 GB.

3. Develop the app.

Even if you didn't make a prototype, it should be clear to you by now that the previous steps break down the workload of the developing process neatly and make it easier. Once you have a clear picture of how your app is going to be, it's time to start coding it.

The most important thing to remember when coding your app is leaving room for future improvements. It's more than likely that you'll introduce new features or refine existing ones over time. So you should make sure that you can achieve this without starting from scratch. Separating the app into modules which contain different bits of functionality is the easiest way to maintain and improve an app in the long run. Modularity is the quality of having such modules in your app's source code.

You can easily let the users choose which functionality they want by letting them download separate "features" to the app, which work as modules in the background. It works more like adding extensions to the core product. It also allows you to iteratively revise each part of the app without changing the whole source code. Modularity requires careful planning and a good knowledge of programming so devote your time for it during the learning period and while you're coding the app.

You should test each module or functionality individually while coding them. You might want to use some dummy data and check if they produce the desired results. When you're sure things are working properly, it's time to integrate them with the core product. Use the device emulators in Xcode and Android Studio to test your app on the go.

One should also take necessary steps to protect user data. Both Android and iOS are quite secure themselves, having device lock settings and user identification methods. Still, it's better to manually implement explicit security features within your app. If you know that the target devices have fingerprint readers (like the iPhone 5s and Samsung Galaxy S5 onwards), then try to integrate them with your app for extra security. The Galaxy S5 & S6 duo have fingerprint scanners certified by PayPal for use with their services. Even Iris scanners will be available on smartphones in the near future. A good developer is updated about the latest trends of the tech world. It gives him an edge to make use of the state of art hardware features. Plus it gives him time to plan ahead for changes that might occur in the future.

Features like user information storage, analytics and push notifications require a backend and there are a number of options you can try. Both iOS and Android can make use of the Google Cloud Services with the App Engine working as a backend. Google even allows you to use it for free up to a certain quota, which is great for testing purposes. You can read about using it here. Amazon Web Services and Microsoft Azure are also prominent players in the cloud infrastructure field. Setting up your own server and backend is also possible, but that takes a lot of time and resources which you may not possess as a beginner. The above companies offer a slew of other facilities like testing and data streaming apart from allowing you to set up a backend in virtually no time. It does take a little time to get familiar with their interfaces but that is nothing compared to the time and effort required to set up your own backend. Take a look at them and compare prices before deciding what to do.

4. Testing and Quality Assurance

Once you're done coding the app, it's time to test it for potential errors. Defects in software are known as "bugs" and so the process of removing them is called debugging. Even though you test each part of your app individually while coding it, errors still come up when they're integrated with the rest of the code. An app usually runs through several versions of itself before finally getting into the hands of the users. These are as follows.

- Prototype – made to demonstrate what you have in mind in the early stages of the SDLC. Acts as a proof of concept.

- Alpha – is the app after its core functionality has been coded but not tested. May contain serious flaws. This version is rarely released to the outsiders, only the developer works with it. A selected group of alpha testers may be employed sometimes.

- Beta – final bits of lower level functionality have been added and is stripped of major bugs. This is the version released for testing to the outsiders.

- Release Candidate – has been tested for all kinds of bugs and fixed as many as possible. Once the developer is satisfied with the quality of the app and certain of its behaviour, he may release it. This version is aptly named the release candidate.

Alpha testing occurs both simultaneous to and at the end of the development stage of the app. This checks for issues in its core functionality. These are usually straightforward bugs which are immediately fixed by the developer. Then comes the beta stage of the app. There are many tricky and invisible bugs that cannot be tested for by the developer alone. These usually occur in the secondary or lower levels of app's functionality. To check for them efficiently, beta testers are called in.

Alpha testing and small parts of beta testing can be done with the tools provided by Apple and Google. These include the device simulators, The Monkey programme for Android and Automation Instrument of Apple. You can run the app in the device simulator and throw random user interactions at it through the two tools above to get log reports on app crashes, resource usage etc. But the device simulator doesn't exactly mimic the real world performance of an actual physical device; resource allocation and certain other features are handled differently. That is why it's better to use an actual device as often as you can.

Beta testing is the more prominent step of testing your app for bugs. Both companies offer extensive support on beta testing for registered developers. Google offers facilities for alpha/beta testing and staged rollouts through its Developer Console. Even if you're not registered with a Publisher account, you can still make use of Google's Testing and Debugging guides under Workflow in the developer tools guides. One thing to keep in mind is enabling Developer Options in the physical devices you use. A new service for testing purposes called the Cloud Test Lab was announced at the Google IO 2015 as coming in the following summer. This allows developers to test their apps on the top 20 Android devices around the world and get crash reports from actual devices. Short videos of the app crashes will also be given with the logs to help developers figure out where the bugs are.

Note – you should create a debug build for testing purposes in the Android Studio with debug keys. A key is a digital signature with a certificate that identifies the author of the app. Don't panic, you can self-sign your certificates, no certification authority needed. Refer the section about generating an APK under releasing and maintaining your app below.

In the case of iOS apps, Apple has a beta test programme called TestFlight which lets you invite users to test your app before releasing it to the App Store. There are a number of steps in distributing pre-release versions using iTunes Connect which you can read at the Beta Testing page of the App Distribution Guide. Again, refer to the exporting section for iOS apps under release procedures below.

Up to a thousand beta testers can be invited directly by providing their email addresses. There are special procedures for exporting a beta version of your app with profiles for testing purposes. But denoting all of them isn't possible within the scope of this book so you should definitely refer the online documentation. This is why we've given so many links here.

Many companies now let independent developers and outsiders take part in beta testing of their software. These are called public beta tests, and participants get access to developer previews of the software. Examples include the beta tests of Windows 10 and iOS 9. People can voice their concerns with the software and ask to change them through these programmes, which give birth to mostly bug-free release versions with which the majority is happy.

When you release an app, people use it in a thousand and one ways that you didn't even think about while making it. Needless to say, this means they're likely to run into all sorts of errors in their user scenarios. Most of these errors can be found and eliminated by public beta test programmes like the above. So how do you conduct a public beta, or at least something like it?

Well, the easiest method is to hire a group of people to test your app. If you can get twenty to thirty friends to test it for free then great! But if that's not possible, try placing a job posting on Craigslist or a freelancer website to hire a small group of beta testers. Let them play with your app for about two weeks and get their reports on the app's behaviour, screenshots of app crash logs etc. Ask them to experiment with the location-based functions, fingerprint reader (and other sensors if any), integration with other system elements like the camera, gallery and memory card access, notification lights, check RAM usage, unusual behaviours like the device heating up while using the app, data fetching from the backend servers etc. There are many college students and unemployed people looking to make a quick buck. Use their feedback to eliminate the bugs in the app and refine it.

Note that you can simply give the apk file of an Android app to someone else to try it out, but iOS testing is a little more strict – you need to get their email addresses and let them download the setup through Apple's beta testing programme. In the case of giving the apk file, Android normally does not let users install apps from unknown sources. They are bound to the app stores by default. But this can be easily changed by enabling Unknown Sources in the Security menu under Settings. You should ask beta testers to check if they've done so. But even if they haven't, Android usually prompts users to change the setting when they try to install apks from the wild.

Ensure these facts to conclude the testing;

1. Core functionality established to work as intended.

2. Backend features work seamlessly with network connection.

3. Functionality based on device's sensors work without hiccups.

Try using the app with such sensors turned off and check how it behaves.

1. All UI elements perform their tasks, both in portrait and landscape modes.

2. The app doesn't randomly crash.

3. It works across all the target devices and OS versions.

This last step can only be ensured by testing the app on as many devices as possible. You can see the importance of carefully selecting a group of beta testers with different devices running different OS versions of the target platform. A variation in screen size is also required. If you want your app to run on devices with Android Jelly Bean and higher, select at least 10 people running Jelly Bean (4.1, 4.2 and 4.3 – there are three Jelly Bean versions), 5-7 each running KitKat and Lollipop.

Once you're sure the app is stable enough to release (or just sick of testing), you can prepare the app for publishing. This involves special steps for each of Android and iOS so we'll talk about them separately.

5. Release and maintain your app.

When the app looks ready to be released, there are a few things you should check and confirm before actually releasing it. Tasks common to both iOS and Android apps are setting the URLs from pre-release test servers to actual backend servers, and removing unused test libraries from your project. The stuff after that are different for each platform. Let's look at Android first.

Android App Release Procedure

We should never release a debug version of the app, as it would give out all sorts of log reports to the user. So first remove all log calls. Then you need to remove the ability to debug the app. This can be achieved by setting the value for *android:debuggable* attribute in the AndroidManifest.xml file to *False*. Alternatively, you can remove it altogether.

Next, we should set proper values for the *android:versionCode* and *android:versionName* parameters in the same XML file. The version code is the internal record of the app's version and is an integer. Later versions of your app should have a higher version code than the former ones. This will allow the app to check if it's the latest version or if an update is available. Then give any string value to the version name. This is used to verbally denote the app's version and will be visible to everyone.

Once you've completed these prerequisites, it's time to generate the APK. But APKs need to be signed with a private key in order to be generated. This identifies its author and brands it under their credentials. Generating a signed APK can be done in two modes, namely Debug and Release. Their names suggest their purposes.

- Debug mode builds APKs for testing purposes and no app market will accept an app built this way. The Android Studio automatically creates certificates and signs the APK when we're debugging the app within the IDE. You can manually create a debug build and share it with testers.

- Release mode creates the file you can actually distribute via the Play Store. We need to provide our own certificate and sign the APK with a private key which will identify us. As mentioned before, we can sign our own certificate.

So how do you generate the APK in any mode? Go to the *Build* menu and click on *Generate Signed APK*. The first time you do this, the *Create New* button will help you to make a new key store, certificate and sign your app. First provide the necessary details in the dialog box that pops up and create the key store. The important things to remember are the path of the key store, its password and the key's password. A validity period of 25 is automatically assigned to the key. You're free to change it, but 25 is the recommended value. More importantly, remember where you keep the key store and keep a backup. If you lose it, you won't be able to update the apps signed with it! You can use this or any other existing key store the next time you try to generate an APK.

Next, select the build mode for the APK you're trying to generate - debug or release. Choose Release mode to create the final setup file.

The next step is uploading it to the Play Store. To do this, log into your Developer Console and click *Add new application* which is near the top of the screen. Follow the onscreen instructions to upload your APK and release it. Here's a bit of further reading on the matter.

iOS App Release Procedure

Similar to the debug and release builds in Android, iOS has two modes for testing and distributing apps. These work under a structure called Signing Identities. There are two of them – *iOS Development* and *iOS*

Distribution. Both include a private key and a certificate unique to the developer.

- iOS Development signing identity allows you to develop and beta test an app in the Apple ecosystem. An app must be signed with a developer signing identity to be tested on a physical device.

- iOS Distribution is the signing identity used to release an app via the App Store.

These identities can be created through the Xcode under the *Preferences* menu. You'll need an active internet connection for the next few steps to complete. Select *Accounts* from the tab icons and then select your Apple ID from the list on the left. You can add it by clicking on the small plus icon to the bottom left corner, if you haven't done so already. Next click on *View Details* on the right side of the window. A dialog box containing signing identities related to your Apple ID will appear. You might have created a development signing identity at the beginning, and if you did, it will be listed under Signing Identities. Click the plus icon below it to add a new iOS Distribution signing identity.

After that, there are 4 steps to release your app to the App Store.

1. Assigning your app to a team.

2. Creating an app record in iTunes Connect.

3. Archiving, validating and submitting your app to iTunes Connect.

4. Submitting the app for review.

The first step is assigning the app to a team. Each and every iOS app needs to be associated with a team, even if it's just one-man with only the developer. To do this, select the project name in the Project Navigator. The project settings panel should come up now. Select the *General* tab and expand the *Identity* section underneath it. There you will see the option to select a team. Click on the drop down icon and select your name. If it isn't already there, you should click Add an account and provide your Apple ID registered for the Apple Developer Programme. Xcode will automatically create a team provisioning profile after that.

In the *General* tab, the Version number should be a two-period-separated list of positive integers, such as 3.4.1 where 3 is a major revision, 4 a minor revision and 1 a maintenance release. This will be shown as the version in the App Store. The build string is a similar list of positive integers representing an iteration of the same bundle.

After that you need to enter a record for your new app in the iTunes Connect portal. Log into iTunes Connect with your Apple ID and go to the My Apps section. Click on the plus sign to the left and select *New iOS App*. Fill in the details carefully, especially the bundle ID and version number. These should be the same as the values seen above Team in the *General* tab above. You can set anything you like for SKU, or the Stock Keeping Unit. It's kept for inventory tracking purposes by the App Store, like app downloads.

Archiving your app is the next compulsory step in releasing the app. Select *Archive* under the *Product* menu of Xcode to do this. If the option is inaccessible (i.e. greyed out), it's probably because the run target selected in the Xcode toolbar is the simulator. Change this to a connected physical iOS device or simply choose iOS Device to access archiving. It will bundle your app and build it so that it's ready for validation.

Next select the archive you just created in the Archives list in the *Organizer* window and click on *Validate*. Choose the team in the dialog box that appears and review the app's details. If prompted, provide the login details of your Developer Programme account. When you continue, Xcode will connect with iTunes Connect and cross-reference the archive with the same-named app record you made earlier. Next it will conduct a validation check on the archived app and will show any errors that come up. Revise your app and repeat the above steps until the validation process succeeds.

Once the archive has been successfully validated, click on *Submit to App Store* in the *Organizer* window. You will be asked to provide the Developer Programme credentials and then the validated archive will be uploaded to iTunes Connect.

When the upload is completed you can see the uploaded version under *Versions* of the relevant app record in *My Apps* of iTunes Connect. Before you submit it for reviewing, you should configure the options under the tabs *Pricing, In-App Purchases* etc. appropriately. Uploading screenshots of the app is also compulsory. You can also organize a beta test through the *Prerelease* tab. Once you're done with these tasks, then select the proper version and click *Submit for Review*. Then comes the long wait until the green light from Apple. The review process usually takes a week or more to send you the results, which will be delivered via email. If the app is rejected, you'll need to look into the issues mentioned in the app and upload a new version to be reviewed.

<u>Bonus Marketing Strategies for Your App</u>

Table of Contents

Introduction

It was way back in August 1994 that the first smartphone was introduced onto the market. Although not referred to as a smartphone, *Simon* as it was called contained functionality which enabled emails and faxes to be sent from the device. Additionally it contained apps for an address book, calendar, note pad, and a calculator, as well as several others apps.

Today there are well over a million apps on the market. Their proliferation can be partly attributed to the monumental growth and popularity of the smartphone, and our fascination with apps. Apple announced at their 2014 Developers' Conference that having also reached the 1.2 million mark for the number of apps on its platform, that their iOS App Store had caught up with its main competitor Google. These are amazing numbers, but you now need to understand that it is not just developed countries which have a fascination for smartphones and apps. While it is reckoned that two thirds of the population in the USA has a smartphone, it is also estimated that half the population in countries with an emerging economy also own a smartphone.

For this reason it is not surprising that developing apps has become big business, and that the number of app developers has increased exponentially. Yet, due to the number of apps and app developers, the problem exists in how to get your app noticed and stand out from all the other apps available. Having toiled hard to develop what you believe to be an amazing app, you want it to become popular. But how do you make your intended users aware of its availability and choose to download it without you needing to spend a fortune on marketing?

Chapter 1 - The Basics

Although the iTunes App Store and the Google Play App Store are the two largest app stores marketing apps, there are other app stores that you should consider using when formulating your marketing strategy. For example you might want to consider the NOOK app store, the Kindle app store, and SlideME for instance.

The first thing to do is to identify your target market and work out a budget for your marketing campaign. Some app stores charge a substantial fee to become a member. This is money which may not be worth your while spending if your app does not fit in with the type of apps that the members of these stores tend to buy.

If you have developed and received approval for an Apple iPhone app you will naturally want to promote it in the iTunes App store as it has such a large number of visitors. There are guidelines on the way that you can promote your app on iTunes which are well documented on their site, and which you need to take heed of. However, before you promote your app anywhere, ensure that it has been rigorously tested. Its appearance should be appealing, and it should have a good name and description. Remember that due to the number of apps available, your potential buyers will spend little time reviewing your app. Therefore it is imperative that make your app catch their eye. Furthermore, as with any other type of marketing campaign you need to keep track of its success rate. There are plenty of marketing analytics tools in existence including Google Analytics for Mobile Apps, and which have been specifically designed to provide data on the marketing efforts of mobile apps. If you fail to use such tools you are not going to be able to fully recognize your ideal buyers or the platforms on which to concentrate your marketing efforts.

Irrespective of whether you are looking to catch the eye of the passionate iPhone users constantly on the look out for new apps for their iPhones, iPods, iPads, and now their iWatches, or whether you have developed an Android app, you need to ensure that you have got the basics right:

- Icon – these need to be well designed and eye catching. The icon should tell the user what the app is designed for, and help to build your brand. It is such an important selling point for any app that if you are in doubt of your ability to create a great icon for your app, then it is worth considering employing a graphics designer to do this for you.

- Description – the description that you write for your app must provide detailed information about your app. Even more importantly it also needs to be written to in such a way that it excites the reader. Before writing your description it is a must that you take the time to carry out some keyword research for SEO purposes. To do this you can type your main keyword into the Google Store Search which will return synonyms for you to use. The Google Adwords keyword tool is also a useful tool to carry out research for keywords to use for SEO purposes as is Straply.com.

Another important point to remember is that when using the keywords that you have selected to use in your description you should not over use them. If you fill your description full of keywords it will likely be considered as spam by the various spam filters. Therefore it is best to use only three to four key words in your description with a density of around 3%. However, the underlining fact still remains; it is the amount of downloads, and especially over a 24 hour period, that will boost your ranking the most. This highlights the need to plan your marketing strategy so that coverage of the release of your app happens in the same time period.

- Website – no business should be without a website, and whether you are developing apps which are free, or in order to earn an income, you must have a website. If you develop your website correctly it should generate plenty of downloads for your apps. There are many ways to attract visitors to your site, well thought out SEO being the first priority. However there are now so many websites in existence you need to do more than just rely on people finding your site by chance.

- Quora, Reddit and other similar sites are useful sites to sign up to. These sites are popular and you should use them to answer questions in your particular field, and to post useful content to help build your reputation and exposure to your brand. On your own website you can also create a blog enabling you to create articles that help to promote your app, and you will want to add prominent buttons so that visitors are encouraged and able to download the app.

Alternatively, rather than having a blog on your website, you may want to create a completely separate site for your blog. This has an added advantage in that you are able to promote your app and enable visitors to download your app in two different places.

When writing the content and articles for your blog, ensure that your content is engaging and interesting. You should avoid writing articles which just promote your apps, although you should try to select topics which enable you to make a mention of them. Also try to include pictures and images in your articles as studies have shown that these are helpful when attempting to engage customers and followers.

There is however one slight downside to separating your blog from your website. By doing so, it does means that you will have two sites to manage and SEO.

- Email Marketing - you can collect the email addresses of your users via your website or blog and via features inside your app. Having the email addresses of your users or potential clients provides you with the ability to send them a newsletter or email whenever you have something noteworthy to announcement such as an update to your app, the release of a new app, or a special that you may be running.

Chapter 2 - Location Based Marketing

As alluded to earlier, there are literally millions of new clients to be found in countries with emerging economies. Take Africa for example of which there seems to be a huge misconception due to the media seemingly only being interested in reporting famines, wars and poverty. However, the number of mobile phone subscribers in Africa was reported to be 635 million in 2014, and is forecasted to reach 930 million by 2019. Due to the lack of land lines, electricity, and the sheer size of the continent, mobile phones have become part of everyday life. Africa missed out on the Internet revolution and laptops, but in terms of mobile users they will soon only be second to China. You will rarely see a young African without a smartphone, and they like their apps and know how to use them. Kenyans for instance have had mobile money since 2007 thanks to the M-Pesa app.

You therefore should explore the possibility of promoting your app in local markets. For example, although Google Play is not available in China, Baidu is, and it is an excellent platform to market your app.

In many cases this will require you to add languages to your app. However, before translating the whole app, to begin with you may just want to consider only translating your app's market description and the metadata used for SEO purposes. This will enable you to determine whether your app might be popular for your targeted audience or specific country. If when reviewing how well your marketing campaign is going, a review of the demographics, i.e. the languages and countries, will indicate whether it may be worth you fully localizing your app. If this is not something that you feel comfortable doing yourself, there are numerous companies such as OneSky and ICcanLocalize who will provide this service for you.

Chapter 3 - Using Social Media

To ignore social media when marketing your app would be a big mistake, but using social media for marketing purposes can be a time consuming job. Therefore rather than attempting to have a presence on every major social media platform, research which of the various platforms are favoured by your intended app user.

Facebook is the most likely platform that will help you to spread the word about your app, and best of all it is free. You should create a Facebook fan page which by default will be publicly visible. Even without a Facebook account visitors will be able to view your photos and updates. You may even want to consider importing an RSS feed from your Twitter account or a blog if you have one, and also set up a discussion forum.

While on the subject of Facebook, given that over 1.4 billion people use Facebook it can also be a successful place advertisements for your app. One of the major benefits of Facebook adverts is that you are able to select the target audience for your advert. Facebook enables you to select the location, age, gender, languages, interests, the types of devices that are used by those people who you want to see your advert. This means that you are only paying to advertise to people who you consider may actually be interested in your app.

YouTube has become one, if not the most popular forms of social media. You therefore should have your own personal YouTube channel where you can promote your apps. It is a simple fact that today's generation of consumers prefer video advertising more than any other form of advertising. However, what you produce needs to be interesting and grab the attention of the viewers. If you succeed in doing this, as with other forms of social media there is the likelihood that your video will be shared, thus further increasing the exposure of your app. Remember also to place your video on your website, and you can promote it further via other forms of social media such as Facebook, Twitter, and Google plus for instance.

Twitter is another social media platform that you should definitely consider using to market your app. Like Facebook Twitter also offers adverts and provides the necessary functionality to target a specific audience for your advert. Furthermore, it is now possible when setting up your adverts on Twitter to request them to run over the Twitter Publisher Network. This means that not only does your advert get seen on Twitter, it also can access the thousands of apps and devices that the MoPub's mobile advertising exchange reaches.

Twitter have also got a function called Twitter Cards, and they have developed one especially for apps. With a <u>Twitter App Card</u> you are able add the name, description and icon of the app, and also highlight its attributes such as its rating and price. Twitter automatically creates App Cards for Tweets which contain a link to either the iTunes App Store App Store or Google Play.

Naturally the more followers you have on Twitter the more exposure you can give to your app. To gain the correct type of followers, you should find out who are the most influential and followed Twitter users in the app industry, and you should follow them also. Join in with their chats as this will allow you to meet and engage with others like-minded people and learn from them. Once you become a known and trusted follower you will quickly increase the number of your own followers.

Another method is to find the followers of your own followers as they are likely to have similar interests to your followers. There are tools such as <u>Tweepi</u> which can provide you with a list of the Twitter accounts that are following your own followers.

Using Twitter also provides you with the ability to respond quickly to any queries or complaints that users may have regarding your app. By providing swift customer support you will build your reputation as a dependable app developer.

Instagram and Pinterest are both leading visual social media platforms and you can use them to display photos that illustrate your app and the people behind it.

There are other social media platforms that you may wish to consider, but remember that they all take up time to manage. If you find this to be the case, using a tool such as <u>Hootsuite</u> will save you much time. Again, do not forget to consider markets further afield. There are some large social media platforms such as <u>renren</u> in China and <u>Mxit</u> in South Africa, which you can use to help market your app in specific countries.

Having taken the time and effort to market your app using social media, you should measure your success and the amount of followers you have gained. This will help you to determine the type of content and which platforms are working best for you. There are numerous sites which you can use to measure the impact of your marketing efforts. <u>Kred</u> and <u>Klout</u> are both noteworthy sites. While Kred only measures your impact on Facebook and Twitter, Klout on the other hand measures your impact on Instagram and Foursquare as well.

Another trick is to look for apps similar to yours which have been successful. Once identified, you can then research what marketing strategy was used to gain their success.

Chapter 4 - Review Sites

Getting reviews of your app will increasing your brand recognition and increase your search engine ranking. There are hundreds of review sites available on the Internet to which you can submit your app for a review. Before spending time doing so, check out the popularity of the review site, and determine if the app that you have developed fits in with the types of apps that they typically review.

When submitting your app for review, ensure that you include all the key information about your app. Review sites receive many requests for reviews, so you need to make sure that the information that you supply is clear and concise otherwise it will likely be ignored.

Many review sites detail exactly the information that you should provide them with before they will consider reviewing your app. If they do not, then you should make sure that you include:

- The name of your app

- Intended audience

- The function of the app, and what makes it stand out from any other similar apps

- Screenshots of the app

- A video of the app

- The links to the app on Google Play and iTunes if applicable

- A link to the app on your own website

- The cost of the app

- A press release for the app

Listed below are some of the most popular review sites to consider, but again do not neglect to submit your app to review sites in emerging countries:

- <u>AppScout</u>

- <u>TechCrunch</u>

- <u>TechRadar</u>

- <u>Cnet Download.com</u>

- <u>TopTen Reviews</u>

Award Sites

Even if you think that your app has no chance of winning an award, do not consider that entering your app to an award site as a waste of time. By participating in app awards you will still benefit from the exposure, reviews, and will generally obtain a good number of downloads.

<u>Conclusion</u>

The app market is highly competitive which is why it is important to plan your marketing campaign. As can be seen, there are numerous ways to market your apps. Some methods are free while others come at a cost. One thing that they all have in common is that they will each take up time if done properly, and you will also need to be patient when looking to see results.

To give your marketing campaign the best chance of success you must set yourself a budget, and research which of the many options available are most likely to work for you. However, if you would rather spend all this necessary time to develop more apps rather than spending it on marketing, then maybe you should consider using the services of an app Marketing Company of which there are many.

<u>Disclaimer</u>

All attempts have been made to verify the information contained in this book but the author and publisher do not bear any responsibility for errors or omissions. Any perceived negative connotation of any individual, group, or company is purely unintentional. Furthermore, this book is intended as a guide and as such, any and all responsibility for actions taken upon reading this book lies with the reader alone and not with the author or publisher. Additionally, it is the reader's responsibility alone and not the author's or publisher's to ensure that all applicable laws and regulations for business practice are adhered to. Lastly, I sometimes utilize affiliate links in the content of this book and as such, if you make a purchase through these links, I will gain a small commission. I have personally used each of the services listed in this book, however, and as such I can say that I would recommend them to my closest friend with the same ease that I now recommend them to you. My opinion is not for sale.